SPORT

THE MOST

AMAZING
HOCKEY
STORIES

100 Inspirational HOCKEY stories and curiosities for kids and young readers The best HOCKEY trivia book ever

PRESENTATION

THIS BOOK IS PART OF **SPORT PLANET** SERIES, AN IMPORTANT AMERICAN PUBLISHING PROJECT SPECIALIZED IN PUBLICATIONS FOR CHILDREN AND YOUNG PEOPLE.

THE SERIES INCLUDES VARIOUS BOOKS WITH A FASCINATING SELECTION OF AMAZING STORIES, FACTS AND CURIOSITIES **ABOUT BASEBALL, FOOTBALL, BASKETBALL, HOCKEY AND VARIOUS SPORTS.**

ALL WITH THE HELP AND ADVICE OF EXPERTS IN THE SECTOR TO ALWAYS PROVIDE HIGH-QUALITY INFORMATION AND CONTENT.

WHAT IS EVEN MORE ATTRACTIVE IS THAT THROUGH THESE BOOKS CHILDREN AND YOUNG PEOPLE WILL IMPROVE THEIR KNOWLEDGE AND LOGICAL CAPABILITIES SIMPLY HAVING FUN. **WHAT'S MORE BEAUTIFUL?**

GOOD READING AND ENJOY.

The Zamboni's Unique Journey

The Zamboni, the ice resurfacing machine used in hockey rinks, has an interesting origin. Frank J. Zamboni invented the machine in 1949. Originally an ice-block vendor, Zamboni was inspired to create the machine to streamline the time-consuming process of resurfacing ice. The Zamboni machine's iconic design and name have become synonymous with maintaining the quality of ice surfaces in hockey arenas around the world.

The Unconventional Hat Trick

In hockey, a "hat trick" refers to a player scoring three goals in a single game. The tradition of throwing hats onto the ice to celebrate a hat trick dates back to the early 20th century. Legend has it that a fan at a Toronto Maple Leafs game in the 1940s threw his hat onto the ice when a player scored three goals. The gesture caught on, and now fans continue to honor players' achievements with a literal shower of hats.

The Stanley Cup's Surprising Beginnings

The Stanley Cup, the ultimate prize in professional ice hockey, has an intriguing origin. It was originally purchased in 1892 by Sir Frederick Arthur Stanley, the Governor General of Canada, as a gift for Canada's top amateur hockey team. The cup evolved into a championship trophy, and today it's awarded to the National Hockey League (NHL) champions. What's remarkable is that the Cup doesn't stay in a museum; each year, the winning team's players and staff take turns hosting it, leading to some exciting and unconventional adventures.

Goalie Mask Evolution

In the early days of hockey, goaltenders didn't wear masks to protect themselves from flying pucks and sticks. The first goalie to wear a mask in an NHL game was Jacques Plante of the Montreal Canadiens in 1959. Plante's innovation was met with resistance from coaches and even teammates, but his success with the mask eventually led to its widespread adoption. Today, goalie masks are not only protective gear but also a canvas for artistic expression, with goalies showcasing unique designs that reflect their personalities.

The Mighty Ducks' Impact

The success of the 1992 movie "The Mighty Ducks," which depicted a youth hockey team's journey to the championship, had a significant impact on hockey's popularity in the United States. The film's heartwarming story and engaging characters resonated with audiences, leading to increased interest in youth hockey programs across the country. The movie even inspired the creation of the real-life Anaheim Ducks NHL team, named after the film's fictional team. This cinematic journey played a part in bringing hockey to a wider American audience.

Bobby Orr's Flying Goal

Bobby Orr, a legendary defenseman, is known for one of the most iconic moments in hockey history. In the 1970 Stanley Cup Finals, he scored the championship-winning goal in overtime for the Boston Bruins. The image of Orr soaring through the air after scoring the goal has become an enduring symbol of hockey greatness and athleticism.

Wayne Gretzky's Record-Breaking Prowess

Wayne Gretzky, often referred to as "The Great One," holds numerous records in hockey, including the most points scored in an NHL career. What's remarkable is that if you removed all his goals from his career, he would still have the most points solely from his assists. His exceptional vision, passing, and playmaking abilities made him a true hockey icon.

The Original Six Teams

The NHL's Original Six teams are the Boston Bruins, Chicago Blackhawks, Detroit Red Wings, Montreal Canadiens, New York Rangers, and Toronto Maple Leafs. These teams formed the league's foundation and played a significant role in shaping the sport's history. The rivalries and history among these teams continue to be celebrated by fans today.

Outdoor Winter Classics

The NHL's Winter Classic is an annual outdoor game held on New Year's Day. The tradition started in 2008 and has featured iconic matchups played in iconic outdoor venues, like football and baseball stadiums. These games allow players and fans to experience hockey in a unique and nostalgic setting, with snowfall, cold temperatures, and open-air excitement.

10

Herb Brooks and the "Miracle on Ice"

The "Miracle on Ice" is one of the most unforgettable moments in sports history. In the 1980 Winter Olympics, the United States ice hockey team, led by coach Herb Brooks, defeated the heavily favored Soviet Union team. The victory was not only a remarkable sports achievement but also a symbol of national pride during a tense Cold War era. The underdog story still resonates as a testament to the power of teamwork and determination.

11

Hockey's Connection to Canada's Identity

Hockey is often considered Canada's national sport, deeply woven into the country's cultural fabric. The sport's origins can be traced back to early indigenous stick-and-ball games. The popularity of hockey in Canada has shaped the nation's identity and values, with many communities embracing the sport as a vital part of their heritage.

The Mighty Penalty Shot

The penalty shot is a dramatic and high-stakes moment in hockey. It's awarded to a player who is fouled on a breakaway scoring opportunity. The player gets a one-on-one chance against the opposing goalie. One of the most famous penalty shots occurred in the 1994 Stanley Cup Finals when New York Rangers' captain Mark Messier converted a crucial penalty shot en route to winning the championship.

13

The Emergence of Women's Hockey

While men's hockey has been prominent for decades, women's hockey has also made remarkable strides. The sport gained international recognition when women's ice hockey was included in the Winter Olympics in 1998. Since then, the competition and skill level have grown significantly, with women's hockey players becoming inspirational role models for aspiring athletes.

14

The Unsung Heroes - Hockey Equipment Managers

Behind every successful hockey team are dedicated equipment managers. These individuals are responsible for ensuring players' gear is prepared, maintained, and ready for every game. Their meticulous work goes beyond just setting up the locker room; they play a pivotal role in ensuring players are comfortable, safe, and prepared to perform at their best.

15

Mario Lemieux's Comeback

Mario Lemieux, a hockey legend, overcame significant challenges during his career. After battling Hodgkin's lymphoma in 1993, he made a triumphant return to the NHL and continued to excel on the ice. His resilience and skill earned him the nickname "Super Mario" and inspired countless fans around the world.

The International Appeal of the NHL

The NHL boasts a diverse array of players from around the world. Players come from various countries, contributing to the league's global appeal. The league's cultural diversity has enriched the game and led to exciting cross-border rivalries, making hockey a true international spectacle.

The Overtime Thrill

Overtime in hockey brings an extra layer of excitement. In the NHL, regular-season overtime rules have evolved, from five-on-five to the current three-on-three format. This change has led to faster-paced, high-intensity endings to tied games, often resulting in breathtaking goals and highlight-reel plays.

The Power of the "Celly"

The post-goal celebration, or "celly," is a unique aspect of hockey culture. Players creatively express their joy and enthusiasm after scoring. From fist pumps to choreographed routines, these celebrations showcase players' personalities and create memorable moments that fans eagerly anticipate.

19

The Pioneering Willie O'Ree

Willie O'Ree broke barriers as the first black player in the NHL when he made his debut with the Boston Bruins in 1958. His courage and perseverance paved the way for diversity and inclusion in the sport. O'Ree's legacy is celebrated annually on January 18th as "Willie O'Ree Day" to honor his contributions to hockey and social progress.

The Curious Case of the "Gordie Howe Hat Trick"

Named after the legendary Gordie Howe, a "Gordie Howe Hat Trick" occurs when a player records a goal, an assist, and a fight in a single game. This unique combination highlights the diverse skills and physicality required in hockey. While not as common as regular hat tricks, achieving a Gordie Howe Hat Trick is a testament to a player's all-around contributions.

21

The Mystery of the "Original Six" Name

The term "Original Six" refers to the six NHL teams that formed the league's core before expansion in 1967. Despite its widespread use, the origin of the phrase remains unclear. Some attribute it to former NHL President Clarence Campbell, while others believe it was a marketing term. Regardless of its origin, the "Original Six" teams hold a special place in hockey history.

The Secret Behind the Slap Shot

The slap shot is one of the most powerful and iconic shots in hockey. Its origin can be traced back to the 1920s when players like Howie Morenz experimented with a new technique involving swinging the stick from behind the body to generate speed and force. Today, mastering the slap shot requires a combination of technique, timing, and raw power.

The Great Equipment Debate - Wooden Sticks vs. Composite Sticks

The evolution of hockey sticks is a fascinating journey. Traditionally made from wood, sticks have evolved with the introduction of composite materials. While wooden sticks have a classic feel, composite sticks offer benefits like increased durability and lighter weight. The ongoing debate between players about the merits of each type highlights the intricacies of equipment preference in the sport.

The Tradition of Playoff Beards

The tradition of growing playoff beards among hockey players is a quirky and unifying ritual. Players often refrain from shaving during the playoffs, creating a distinctive and often scruffy look. The origin of the tradition is believed to date back to the 1980s with the New York Islanders, and it has since become a symbol of a player's commitment and unity during the intense playoff season.

The Birth of the Blue Line

The blue line, a fundamental element of hockey rinks, serves as a boundary between offensive and defensive zones. It was introduced in 1918 to prevent players from "goal-hanging" near the opponent's net. This innovation transformed the game, adding strategic depth and influencing offensive and defensive tactics.

The Legend of "Boom Boom" Geoffrion

Bernie "Boom Boom" Geoffrion, a Hall of Fame player, earned his nickname from his powerful slap shot that echoed like a boom. Geoffrion's contributions extended beyond his skills; he's credited with popularizing the practice of curving hockey sticks for enhanced shooting. His impact on the game's equipment and style remains influential.

The Mystique of Hockey Sweaters

Hockey jerseys, often called "sweaters," hold a special place in the hearts of players and fans. Teams' logos, colors, and designs create a sense of identity and community. The tradition of swapping jerseys after games as a sign of respect and camaraderie adds a unique touch to the sport's sportsmanship.

The Elevation of Hockey Analytics

Advanced statistics, or "analytics," have become integral to modern hockey strategy. These metrics offer insights into player performance, team tactics, and game dynamics. The widespread use of analytics has transformed how coaches, analysts, and fans understand the game, leading to smarter decision-making and innovative strategies.

The Unexpected Emergence of Goaltender Goals

Goaltenders, traditionally known for their defensive skills, have occasionally surprised everyone by scoring goals. Martin Brodeur, a Hall of Fame goalie, holds the NHL record for most career goals scored by a goaltender. These rare moments of goaltender offense add excitement and unpredictability to the game.

The Innovations of the "Hockey Night in Canada" Theme

The "Hockey Night in Canada" theme song is one of the most recognizable tunes in sports broadcasting. Written in 1968 by Dolores Claman, the tune became synonymous with Saturday night hockey in Canada. Its catchy melody and connection to the sport's heritage have made it an enduring part of hockey culture.

The Art of Stickhandling

Stickhandling, the skill of controlling the puck with a hockey stick, is a delicate and mesmerizing aspect of the game. Players use quick wrist movements, agile footwork, and precise hand-eye coordination to maneuver the puck past opponents. Mastering stickhandling requires finesse and creativity, adding a touch of artistry to the sport.

The Olympic Hockey Drama

The Winter Olympics offer a unique stage for international hockey competition. The absence of NHL players in some tournaments, such as the 2018 Olympics, sparked discussions about the significance of representing one's country and showcased talented players from various leagues around the world.

The Evolution of Goaltender Masks

The transformation of goaltender masks from rudimentary face protection to intricate designs is a testament to safety advancements and personal expression. Jacques Plante's decision to wear a mask in 1959 marked a turning point, leading to the development of safer and more creative designs that reflect a goaltender's individuality.

The Impact of "Sudden Death" Overtime

"Sudden death" overtime, where the first team to score wins, adds intense drama to hockey games. Introduced in the NHL in 1983, it heightened excitement and urgency in tied games. Sudden-death goals have the power to instantly change a team's fate, creating unforgettable moments of triumph and heartbreak.

The Mystery of the Hat Trick's Origin

While the tradition of throwing hats on the ice to celebrate a hat trick is well-known, the origin of the term itself is debated. One theory suggests that fans in the 1800s used to collect money in their hats to reward players who scored three goals. Another theory involves a restaurant owner gifting a hat to players achieving the feat. Regardless of its origin, the term has become an integral part of hockey culture.

The Innovations in Goalie Equipment

Goaltender equipment has come a long way from the early days of minimal protection. Innovations in materials and design have led to safer and more effective gear. However, debates about the size of equipment and its impact on scoring have been ongoing, prompting adjustments by the NHL to balance safety and competitive balance.

The Tradition of Playoff Overtime

Playoff overtime in hockey is a unique and thrilling experience. Unlike the regular season's shootout format, playoff games continue with sudden-death overtime until a team scores. The tension, exhaustion, and elation of a game-winning playoff overtime goal contribute to the unparalleled drama of postseason hockey.

The Enigmatic "Selke Trophy"

The Frank J. Selke Trophy is awarded annually to the NHL's best defensive forward. Named after Frank J. Selke, a former general manager, the award highlights players who excel in defensive play, penalty killing, and overall two-way performance. The focus on defensive skills adds depth to recognizing players' contributions beyond scoring.

The Rise of Hockey Analytics Websites

Hockey analytics websites and statistics platforms have become essential resources for fans, analysts, and teams. Websites like Corsica, Natural Stat Trick, and Hockey-Reference provide in-depth insights into player performance, on-ice trends, and advanced metrics, transforming how the game is understood and discussed.

The Traditions of Playoff Beards and "No-Shave November"

The tradition of playoff beards has an office counterpart in "No-Shave November." During the playoffs, players grow beards as a symbol of unity and superstition. Similarly, "No-Shave November" encourages men to grow facial hair to raise awareness for cancer-related causes. Both traditions showcase how sports and societal initiatives can intertwine for a positive impact.

The Evolution of Goalie Masks' Designs

Goalie mask designs have evolved beyond protection to become canvases for creative expression. Artists and players collaborate to design masks that showcase personal stories, team logos, and pop culture references. This artistic dimension adds a unique visual element to the sport and allows goalies to share their personalities with fans.

The International Rivalries of "Canada vs. USA"

The rivalry between Canada and the United States in hockey transcends the border. From international tournaments like the Winter Olympics and World Championships to heated matchups in the NHL, these contests evoke strong national pride and intense competition, creating memorable moments and unforgettable clashes.

43

The Globalization of the NHL

The NHL's player diversity continues to expand, with players hailing from various countries. European and international players have become integral to the league's success, enriching the sport's skillset and showcasing the global reach of hockey.

The Charm of Minor League Hockey

Minor league hockey teams, like those in the American Hockey League (AHL) and ECHL, offer a different perspective on the sport. These teams often have creative and humorous mascots, quirky promotions, and unique fan interactions that create a fun and accessible atmosphere for fans of all ages.

45

The Legend of Bobby Hull's Slap Shot Speed

Bobby Hull, known for his incredible slap shot, was rumored to have one of the hardest shots in hockey history. It's said that his slap shot reached speeds exceeding 118 mph (190 km/h). While precise measurements from his era are unavailable, Hull's reputation for his powerful shot remains a part of hockey folklore.

The Infamous "Flying V" Formation

In the movie "The Mighty Ducks," the fictional youth hockey team employs a unique strategy known as the "Flying V." While the formation is a source of amusement, it's not practical in real hockey games due to its predictability and lack of defensive structure. However, the "Flying V" lives on in pop culture as a memorable representation of hockey in cinema.

47

The "Spin-o-rama" Move

The "spin-o-rama" is a dazzling move used by players to outmaneuver defenders. The player skates towards the net, performs a spin to protect the puck, and then shoots. While the move is aesthetically pleasing, its legality and execution have been subjects of debate, leading to changes in NHL rules to clarify its use in shootouts.

The Connection Between Hockey and Music

Hockey and music often intersect, with players sharing their musical talents off the ice. Some players are skilled musicians who play instruments like guitar, drums, and piano. The bond between music and hockey extends to pre-game playlists, anthems, and arena traditions that create a lively and energetic atmosphere.

The Enduring Legacy of Wayne Gretzky's Records

Wayne Gretzky's records and achievements in hockey remain untouchable milestones. His 2,857 career points, 894 career goals, and countless other records set a standard that is unlikely to be surpassed. Gretzky's influence on the game extends beyond statistics, as his impact on player development and the sport's popularity is immeasurable.

The Legendary Goalie Duel

The 1994 Eastern Conference Finals featured an iconic goalie duel between Martin Brodeur of the New Jersey Devils and Dominik Hasek of the Buffalo Sabres. Game 6 of the series lasted for 4 overtime periods, with Brodeur making 49 saves and Hasek making 70 saves. The Devils won 1-0, and the game is remembered as one of the longest and most intense goalie battles in NHL history.

51

The Unconventional "Butterfly" Style

The "butterfly" style of goaltending, popularized by goaltenders like Patrick Roy and Martin Brodeur, revolutionized how goalies play. Instead of staying upright, goalies drop to their knees, spreading their legs to cover the lower part of the net. This technique maximizes net coverage and has become the foundation of modern goaltending.

52

The Fascinating History of the Penalty Box

The penalty box, where players serve time for infractions, has evolved from a simple wooden bench to a specialized area. The concept dates back to the early 20th century when players were banished to the penalty bench. Over time, the penalty box became an integral part of the game, serving as a symbolic reminder of sportsmanship and discipline.

The Invention of the Goal Light

The iconic goal light that illuminates when a goal is scored wasn't always part of hockey. In the early days, referees had to signal goals using a whistle and hand signals. The first electric goal light was introduced in 1956 at the Montreal Forum, enhancing the spectator experience and ensuring everyone knew when a goal was scored.

The Evolution of Hockey Nets

Hockey nets have undergone significant changes over the years. Originally, they were open, and players had to retrieve the puck from the back of the net. In 1912, the first enclosed nets were used, allowing the puck to be easily retrieved from the net's back. Modern nets include features like pegs for secure attachment to the ice and red goal-line indicators for video reviews.

The Birth of the Power Play
The concept of the power play, where one team has a numerical advantage due to a penalty to the opposing team, was introduced to hockey in the early 20th century. This innovation added strategic complexity to the game, requiring teams to capitalize on their extra player while maintaining defensive discipline.

The Mystery of "Puck Over Glass" Penalties

The "puck over glass" penalty, where a player shoots the puck over the glass and into the crowd, results in a delay of game penalty. The rule was implemented in 2005 to prevent teams from intentionally delaying the game. While it's meant to increase the pace of play, the subjectivity of whether a player intentionally shot the puck over the glass sometimes sparks debate among fans and players.

The Tale of the Stanley Cup's Adventures

The Stanley Cup has a history of unconventional adventures. It's been used as a planter, a bowl for dog food, and even accidentally left at the side of a road. These stories showcase the Cup's unique journey as it travels with players, often leading to unexpected and amusing tales.

The Impact of the "Gretzky Rule"

The "Gretzky Rule" refers to a rule change in 1985 that disallowed players to make forward passes with their skates beyond the blue line. This change aimed to curb Wayne Gretzky's uncanny ability to make precise passes while his skates were over the blue line, creating a more balanced playing field.

The Traditions of Playoff Handshakes

After a playoff series, teams participate in a tradition known as the "handshake line," where players from both teams shake hands as a sign of respect and sportsmanship. This tradition reinforces the notion that, despite fierce competition, players share a mutual appreciation for the game and each other's efforts.

The Evolution of Protective Gear

From minimal protection to advanced gear, hockey players' equipment has evolved for safety and performance. Innovations like helmets, visors, and padding have transformed the way players safeguard themselves, enabling them to play with confidence and reduce the risk of injuries.

61

The Legacy of "Mr. Hockey" Gordie Howe

Gordie Howe, often referred to as "Mr. Hockey," left an indelible mark on the sport. Known for his exceptional skill and toughness, Howe played in five decades and held numerous records. His influence extended beyond the ice, as he inspired generations of players and fans with his dedication and sportsmanship.

The Evolution of Ice Surfaces

Hockey's playing surface, the ice, has evolved over the years. Outdoor rinks with natural ice were once common, but the advent of indoor arenas with artificial ice provided controlled conditions and extended playing seasons. Modern technology ensures consistent ice quality, contributing to the fast-paced and exciting nature of the game.

The Role of Mascots in Hockey

Mascots play a unique role in hockey, engaging fans of all ages and adding a fun element to the game. These colorful characters entertain the crowd, participate in games, and create memorable experiences for fans during intermissions and breaks.

The Unpredictability of Shootouts

Shootouts were introduced to the NHL in 2005 to break ties after overtime. The one-on-one showdown between shooter and goaltender adds suspense and excitement, with no guarantee of victory for either side. Shootouts showcase players' skills and nerves, often leading to unexpected outcomes.

The Influence of Hockey Families

Hockey has a rich tradition of families passing down the love for the sport through generations. The Sutters, Staals, and Subbans are just a few examples of families with multiple siblings playing in the NHL. These families' legacies demonstrate the profound impact of shared passion and dedication.

The Phenomenon of "Hat Trick Heroes"
Scoring a hat trick is a remarkable achievement, but some players have taken it a step further by achieving multiple hat tricks in a single game. This exceptional feat, known as a "hat trick of hat tricks," showcases a player's dominant performance and the thrill of witnessing history in the making.

The Tradition of Opening-Night Banners

Many NHL teams raise banners during opening-night ceremonies to celebrate achievements from the previous season. These banners honor accomplishments like division championships, conference titles, and Stanley Cup victories. The tradition sets the tone for the upcoming season and lets fans relive unforgettable moments.

The Hockey Hall of Fame's Treasures

The Hockey Hall of Fame in Toronto is home to a vast collection of artifacts, memorabilia, and exhibits celebrating the history of the sport. From historic jerseys to game-used equipment, the Hall of Fame preserves the legacy of hockey's greatest players, moments, and innovations.

The Art of Shootout Deception

Shootouts require not only skill but also creativity. Players use various moves and fakes to deceive goaltenders and score. From the "Forsberg move" to the "Datsyukian deke," these inventive techniques add an element of showmanship to the game's decisive moments.

The Unforgettable "Miracle at the Met"

The "Miracle at the Met" refers to a 1982 playoff game between the Minnesota North Stars and the Chicago Blackhawks. In a historic showdown, the North Stars scored two goals in just five seconds during the third period, setting an NHL record for the fastest two goals by one team in a playoff game.

The Evolution of NHL Expansion

The NHL has expanded over the years to include teams from various cities and regions. From the "Original Six" era to the present, expansion teams like the Vegas Golden Knights have quickly become competitive and captured the hearts of new fanbases, showcasing the sport's growth.

The Tradition of Captaincy in Hockey

The role of a team captain in hockey is symbolic and essential. Captains lead by example on and off the ice, representing their teams with pride. The tradition of wearing the "C" on the jersey carries a legacy of leadership and sportsmanship that resonates throughout the game.

The Excitement of Overtime Playoff Goals

Playoff overtime goals are celebrated with unmatched euphoria. The sudden-death nature of overtime adds a heightened sense of drama, and each goal can propel a team closer to championship glory. The emotional roller coaster of overtime goals makes them some of the most memorable moments in hockey history.

The Impact of Social Media on Hockey

The rise of social media has transformed how fans engage with hockey. Players, teams, and fans use platforms like Twitter, Instagram, and TikTok to share highlights, connect with the community, and provide behind-the-scenes insights, fostering a new level of interaction and global camaraderie.

The Tradition of Number Retirement

Retiring a player's number is a testament to their impact on a team and the sport. Teams honor legendary players by raising their jersey numbers to the rafters, a gesture that immortalizes their contributions and ensures their legacy lives on for future generations.

The Thrill of Game 7 Drama

Game 7 in a playoff series is the ultimate do-or-die scenario. The winner advances, while the loser's season comes to an end. The pressure, intensity, and uncertainty of Game 7s create unforgettable moments, with players leaving everything on the ice in pursuit of victory.

The Legacy of Women's Hockey Pioneers

Women's hockey has its own set of pioneers who blazed a trail for future generations. Players like Hayley Wickenheiser, Cammi Granato, and Manon Rhéaume broke barriers and championed the growth of women's hockey, inspiring countless young players around the world.

The Influence of Coaching Legends

Coaches like Scotty Bowman, Al Arbour, and Toe Blake have left an indelible mark on the sport. Their strategic brilliance, leadership skills, and ability to motivate players have shaped championship teams and set coaching standards that aspiring coaches still strive to achieve.

The Art of Stick Taping

Stick taping is a ritualistic aspect of hockey, with players meticulously wrapping their sticks for optimal grip and feel. The patterns, colors, and superstitions associated with stick taping make it a personalized and visually distinct element of the game.

The Legendary "Red Army" Team

The Soviet Union's national team, often referred to as the "Red Army" team, was a dominant force in international hockey during the Cold War era. Known for their precision passing and innovative strategies, they challenged North American teams in iconic matchups that transcended sports and politics.

The Mystery of Hockey's "Original Rules"
The earliest versions of hockey were played with a wide range of rules and variations. The first official rules were established in 1875 at McGill University in Canada. These "original rules" set the foundation for the sport's development, paving the way for the standardized rules we see today.

The Dynamic Duo: Forsberg and Sakic

The Colorado Avalanche's Peter Forsberg and Joe Sakic formed a dynamic duo during the late 1990s and early 2000s. Their chemistry on the ice propelled the Avalanche to multiple championships, and their partnership remains a shining example of teamwork and offensive prowess.

The Curious Case of Empty-Net Goals

Empty-net goals occur when a team removes their goaltender for an extra attacker, leaving the net unprotected. While they secure a lead, empty-net goals don't always contribute to a player's statistics. Despite their simplicity, they add suspense to the final moments of a game.

The "Hockey Fights Cancer" Initiative

The NHL's "Hockey Fights Cancer" campaign is a league-wide initiative to raise awareness and funds for cancer research and patient support. Players, teams, and fans unite to show their support, fostering a sense of solidarity and demonstrating the positive impact of sports in raising awareness for important causes.

The Rise of Outdoor Stadium Games

The NHL's outdoor stadium games, like the Winter Classic and Stadium Series, have become iconic events. Played in football and baseball stadiums, these games showcase hockey's roots and provide a unique experience for players and fans, with the elements of weather and large crowds adding to the spectacle.

The "Code" of Hockey Fights

Fighting has been a contentious aspect of hockey's history. The unwritten "code" of fighting involves respecting opponents and knowing when to engage in a fight. While the role of fighting has evolved, it remains a complex and debated aspect of the sport's culture.

The Global Reach of the IIHF World Championships

The IIHF World Championships bring together national teams from around the world. While overshadowed by the Olympics, these tournaments offer a chance for non-NHL players and emerging hockey nations to showcase their skills on the international stage.

The Influence of Hockey Video Games

Hockey video games, like the NHL series by EA Sports, have introduced countless fans to the sport. These games offer a virtual experience that allows players to take control of their favorite teams and players, fostering a deeper connection to the game and its players.

The Historic 1972 Summit Series

The 1972 Summit Series between Canada and the Soviet Union is a landmark moment in hockey history. The eight-game series featured intense competition and cultural significance, symbolizing the rivalry between Eastern and Western ideologies during the Cold War era.

The "One Goal" Mindset

The phrase "one goal" symbolizes a player's laser focus on achieving victory. It reminds players to approach each shift, period, and game with unwavering determination. The concept emphasizes the importance of breaking down larger objectives into smaller, achievable steps.

The Evolution of Hockey Broadcasting
Hockey broadcasting has transformed from radio commentary to high-definition TV broadcasts with multiple camera angles and advanced graphics. The use of technology enhances the viewing experience, bringing fans closer to the action and providing insightful analysis.

The International Impact of NHL Players

NHL players often represent their countries in international tournaments like the Olympics and World Championships. Their participation not only showcases the league's global talent but also fosters international camaraderie and collaboration among players.

The Artistry of Goaltending Masks

Goaltender masks have evolved into canvases for artistic expression. From intricate designs that reflect a player's personality to masks that honor past legends, these pieces of equipment capture the creativity and individuality of goaltenders.

The Drama of Last-Second Goals

Last-second goals are some of the most exhilarating moments in hockey. A goal scored with only seconds remaining can dramatically shift the outcome of a game, leaving fans on the edge of their seats and players in a mix of jubilation and disbelief.

The Tradition of National Anthems

National anthems before games unite players and fans in a display of patriotism and sportsmanship. The anthems' melodies and lyrics evoke a sense of pride, and players often stand side by side, representing their respective countries with respect and unity.

The Mythical "Triple Gold Club"

The "Triple Gold Club" is an exclusive group of players who have won a Stanley Cup, an Olympic gold medal, and a World Championship gold medal. Achieving this feat requires exceptional skill, dedication, and timing due to the rarity of the three major accomplishments aligning.

The Connection Between Hockey and Charity

Many NHL players and teams actively engage in charitable efforts to give back to their communities. Initiatives like player foundations, charity games, and community programs demonstrate how hockey can have a positive impact beyond the ice.

The Impact of Hockey Literature

Hockey literature, including novels, biographies, and historical accounts, offers fans an immersive way to explore the sport's history, culture, and stories. These written works capture the essence of hockey and its significance in the lives of players and fans.

The Everlasting Bond Between Fans and the Game

The relationship between hockey fans and the sport is marked by unwavering passion and dedication. Fans invest emotionally in their favorite teams and players, celebrating victories and enduring defeats together. This bond ensures that hockey's legacy continues to thrive and evolve for generations to come.

100

The Enigmatic Goalie Shutout Record

The record for most shutouts by a goalie in a single NHL season is held by George Hainsworth, who achieved 22 shutouts during the 1928-29 season. This remarkable feat highlights an era when goaltending and defensive strategies were vastly different. In today's game, with increased scoring and advanced equipment, breaking this record remains an extraordinary challenge.

Made in the USA
Monee, IL
22 November 2023

47106803R00060